FRANKLIN
MOORE

FRANKLIN MOORE

A NIGERIAN FATHER

BY

GREGG MOORE

HIS AMERICAN SON

Library of Congress Control Number: 2017909974
ISBN: Hardcover   978-1-5434-3255-8
                    Softcover   978-1-5434-3256-5
                    eBook   978-1-5434-3257-2

Print information available on the last page.

Rev. date: 08/04/2017

To order additional copies of this book, contact:
Xlibris
1-888-795-4274
www.Xlibris.com
Orders@Xlibris.com
760160

CONTENTS

Chief Franklin Moore was an African father and the only son of Sir William Moore and father of many sons and daughters including this author.

Dr. Gregg Moore, an American

Dedication to Oritsema

August 21, 1957–July 16, 2012

She was better known as Olusegun Kukoyi in high school and in the university, even though her full name is Olusegun Oritsema (f) Kukoyi before becoming Mrs. O. O. Adegbeye.

I dedicate this book to her as 'Segun shared the same middle name with my father, Franklin Moore, being born by an Itsekiri mother also. Besides, she shared other attributes with Daddy Frank Oritsemi (m), graduating too from Ibadan, the largest city in West Africa—Saint Anne's School Molete Ibadan vs. Government College, Ibadan.

But Olusegun, Oritsema, now of blessed memory, had some very sterling qualities of her own. She was simple, innocent, and transparent, and became a hardworking professional after graduation and a person who could confront any believer at the then University of Ife (now Obafemi Awolowo University) if she thinks that child of God was not walking right with his or her Heavenly Father. She was a lifelong member of the Student Christian Movement (SCM) and was a happy and joyous mother and housewife.

0. INTRODUCTION

This author writes as one born in British West Africa (though an American) but will try, as hard as this might be, to be American in narrative and language. In disagreeing or having a contrary opinion, the average American merely says "Hell no," but to authenticate what is being said as true, the word *true* doesn't even come up. Some other phrase is used. This is just like what occurred on a morning last October when this book was still in the making. By a football field near my office, I walked by a girl of about twenty and her boyfriend, who I put as twenty-three, with bushy hair. This girl wrapped the boy's hair all around him and around his moustache and described to him who he looked like. Whether it was good or bad, I do not know, but they both did. And to increase the force of her statement, do you know what she said? She said, "I swear to the fucking God."

I once had the story of a student in an exam hall, where the question before him was to write about some specific aspects of the life of the Lord Jesus Christ. But as the story went, this excellent student, given all that happened in class around revision time, had calculated before the actual exam that the essay part of that paper would be on the apostle Paul and so prepared accordingly, based on his permutation, to write an essay on Saint Paul, neglecting other personalities in the biblical times and beyond what could be the content of that section of the exam.

And so in the exam, when this excellent student saw the essay part of question, which he first turned to, he couldn't believe what he saw on the question paper. And because he had overprepared for a particular character in the Bible, he began the story with the introduction, "This paper requests the student to write an essay on Jesus Christ, but who am I to write about my Lord? I will instead write on the apostle Paul."

He wrote so much that even when the time for the whole exam was about to be over, he had not addressed the objective part of the paper and had to submit his paper without the objective section of the examination.

And so the best student scored zero in that very subject where he is the best.

There were two personalities: William A. Moore and Franklin O. Moore. Whereas this author's first preference would have been to write on the life of William Moore, unfortunately, he wasn't born before the former passed on into eternity. But that ought not to be enough reason to prevent a candidate from writing about him, for there are resources and, of course, many people like William Moore's wife, children, and others who were still alive when this author was born and who knew William Moore well enough, even though at the time, this writer had not developed enough interest or the ability to write except in the partial fulfillment of the requirement of degrees like the following:

- "Danfo Agbero Bus Conduct Occupation Group in Lagos: A study in Urban Social Stratification" (1980) for his bachelor's
- "Benefit Analysis of Transferred Securities: Retrieval and Repayment" (1982) (carried out in NAL Merchant Bank) for his first master's—an MBA
- "Maintenance Level among Middle Management in Banks in Lagos" (1988) (study carried out

among middle-level managers in the First Bank of Nigeria in Lagos, Nigeria) for a second master's

- "White Black and Other" (2003), a study wholly carried out in Chicago, in the United States of America, for the award of a Ph D degree in Africa and was later published into a book.

But now, this author has moved into writing just for his reading audience and not in hope for the award of any more degrees, like for instance *Confronting Youth Apathy* (2016) besides all the other essays with the exception of the penultimate and the last had extensive coursework attached to them, with the penultimate having only two course requirements: (i) Advanced Philosophy of the Social Sciences and (ii) the Theory of Knowledge. The last one was written on the suggestion of a reader of his earlier book, whose main concern was the wrong direction he saw our youths going to. Surprisingly, he is neither a psychologist nor a clergyman, but an ordinary American citizen—a bank manager.

In this work, this author chose to write on Franklin Moore as an eyewitness, and maybe he will yet write about Daddy Frank's father, whom he really adores. Yes, maybe. But he should quickly add that he does not expect people in general who will read this book to agree with him, especially those in the very culture in which he grew up and maybe those who hold the same worldview as Daddy Frank did.

Specifically, this author knows somebody who knows Daddy Frank as well as himself who already called for caution in this work—MD—one of Franklin Moore's daughters-in-law. Why really do we write autobiographies? it may be asked. This might be to say what some people already know, and it could also be to keep the memory of others alive, especially those who had passed on to the world beyond. It may also be to be able learn from the lives of others as we have just this one fleeting life—at least in this world—and when it is gone, that is it. We can no longer relive our lives when it is all over. But in particular, this write-up is about a father—fathers, or parents, if you like. What type of father, mother, or parent are you, and what would your children and others remember you for?

1. EARLY UPBRINGING AND ELEMENTARY SCHOOL

Franklin Oritsemi Moore (oritse-esi-utieyin-mi), whose name means "God has my back," was born to Akpieyi and Akpero from the villages of Batere and Jakpa of the Itsekiri Kingdom, respectively, on January 25, 1917, in Warri, Nigeria. Whereas his mother was the last in her family, she was married to the son of a princess, who in turn was married out by the monarch to a foreigner named Akinbo (Akenbo) who had no link to the Itsekiri people talk more of its monarchy, whose only link may as well have been that he was very wealthy, respectable, and influential.

Akenbo (Akinbo) came to the land of the Itsekiri people around the time the white explorers came too from faraway Egba Land in the present Ogun State of

Nigeria, not too distant from Nigeria's former capital, Lagos. And so while he allowed his only son to inculcate the education and ways of the whites, he merely saw the whites as a people of a different culture who could be good for the future, but he ranked his Yoruba-Egba culture, tradition, education, and way of life on equal footing with that of the visitors from over the seas. So William Moore inculcated Western learning and education and enjoyed many benefits that came with his royal maternal blood and enlightenment when a majority of the people, if not all, were illiterates and uneducated. So William-Akpieyi (meaning will not share this—with a foreigner one could guess) automatically took up a representative role for the Itsekiri people before the whites who had come to acquire land and territories of people (re. *The Education of a British-Protected Child* by Chinua Achebe) immediately after obtaining a first-class education at a missionary school in Calabar, Nigeria, the Hope Waddell Training Institution.

But because of the immense responsibility of office and, as this author supposes, the externalities of office— the extreme danger to his family as a result of intertribal fighting between the different tribes in the delta region seeking for a position of prominence before the white overlords—even though William Moore had adequate protection and force, he must have considered it wise and safe to transfer his immediate family away from the battlefield in Warri to a safe haven and distant town of Sapele at the time.

So grandmother Akpero and her three children—two daughters, Georgina and Esther, and a son, Franklin—moved (relocated) to Sapele, where they continued their early life as Frank's two elder sisters, a nurse and a secretary, began to work after their modest training and education in a nation where people were basically primitive and uneducated. But something more was expected from a son—an only son* of William Moore.

Another reason for this relocation, it might be said, was that William Moore's in-laws were people of means with many landed properties in Sapele. As a little boy growing up in Lagos, this author used to think that the only three cities or towns in the then midwestern region of Nigeria were Benin, Sapele, and Warri, but there were many more like Asaba, Ughelli, Abraka, Eku, Ibuzo, and Ozoro, to mention just six.

At what stage in life Daddy Frank's football skills came to be recognized is not clear, but it must have developed locally in the ancient town of Sapele and

---

* This author's finding reveals the likelihood that grandfather William Akpieyi had other sons and daughters by concubine(s) possibly, but since people were generally uneducated, their connection with him was lost.

must have been noticed, though there might not have been serious exposure for that bulging footballer. But on gaining admission to Nigeria's premier college (both at the time and today)—the Government College Ibadan (GCI)—this skill must have been easily noticed to have earned Daddy Frank a spot in the college's first eleven team in the early 1930s.

What happened to Daddy Frank's playmates both in Warri and Sapele while growing up in his preteen and maybe his early teen years, one might wonder, as it seems he did not continue with any of them much later in life. And could it be that a leap he was about to make caused further separation of himself away from his peers at the time, a separation that was already in existence at his birth because of the status of his father, William Moore, in society? Not to mention that his grandmother and grandfather were a princess and affluent-cum-nobility?

2. OFF TO COLLEGE

So Daddy Frank then left Sapele for the largest city in the then West African region—Ibadan—to attend Government College Ibadan (GCI), where most of the children of the whites living in Nigeria then attended. Of course, there must have been some spaces reserved for the children of the wealthiest Nigerians, some for students with scholarships due to their extremely brilliant performance in the entrance examination, etc., most of which, later settled in that ancient city of Ibadan, which for so many years, was the capital of the southwestern region of Nigeria, which in the era before independence, was led by Chief Obafemi Awolowo of Ikenne and Chief Samuel Ladoke Akintola, a.k.a. SLA, of Ogbomosho as his deputy. Of course, the few that came to Ibadan from outside the western region of Nigeria must have returned to their home cities and regions. As for Moore, he had two choices of returning: to Warri, where his father reigned, or to Sapele, where he came from, with his mother and his sisters still there while he was gone away to acquire the golden fleece of education in Ibadan.

Two remarkable things happened while Daddy Frank was at GCI. He got a direction or profession for his life that was distinct and different from that of his father, who was a local administrator, historian, and anthropologist. He became interested in the civil service, and so instead of returning permanently to Warri or to Sapele, he headed for Lagos—the expanding and foremost town of the British protectorate that later became known as Nigeria in the late 1930s. And at what juncture Moore took to accounting may be difficult to know, whether at Government College Ibadan or when he joined the colonial service in Lagos. But there is another plausible theory this author will attempt to advance at this juncture.

While growing up, unlike this author's generation, Daddy Frank and his siblings Georgina and Esther saw, felt, and spoke to their grandfather and felt his influence. He was this rich alien in the Itsekiri Kingdom whose wealth earned him a position of respect and esteem that very soon made him the king's son-in-law. His wealth was observable, felt, and enjoyed. Could it be that it was at this level or juncture in life that Daddy Frank first got his inkling to become a professional accountant while observing how his Granddad Akinbo (Akenbo) managed and controlled resources? So it could be opined, therefore, that before Daddy Frank became a student at the Ibadan premier college, the Government College Ibadan (GCI), he had already braced himself up to pursue the accountancy profession.

3. Occurrence Back Home While in College

Something remarkable happened to Moore while he was a student in Ibadan. It is not difficult to conjecture how Moore skyrocketed into advanced fame, first by being a local football star and now, a college student in the distant town of Ibadan, the largest in the whole West Africa. Women, it has been said, love sports heroes or champions who may then pick and choose any of these fans. Moore was not an exception, and he eventually got a girlfriend in the early 1930s, who eventually became pregnant and had to move in with Moore's immediate elder sister, Miss Esther Boyowa Moore, the secretary, as Moore returned to complete his college education in Ibadan. But an accident, or should I say incident, happened that changed Moore's outlook for life about women—in particular, married women. More on this later, but for now, we could just imagine the scenario of what happened.

The two daughters of William Moore were already graduates, and being literate, with hospital and office jobs as nurse and secretary respectively, they were not home most of the working hours of the day. Georgina Moore might even have been out all night on night duty as a nurse. But as the story went, as told to this author by Aunty Esther herself, every day, she left her pregnant sister-in-law at home as she went to work in the regular hours. The sister-in-law eventually delivered a baby girl. Aunty Georgina Moore, as a trained nurse, must have been involved in the delivery since Daddy Frank was still in college in Ibadan, Nigeria. With time, however, this baby girl died! Yet the young mother continued to stay alone in her sister-in-law's home while her man was away in college in Ibadan. So according to Aunty Esther—later Mrs. Foresythe—she did not know that Franklin's wife had become pregnant again despite the morning sickness signs, etc., until she was alerted by a neighbor who wondered if she was blind! This was because neither she nor her elder sister had been pregnant before.

While everybody was at work and Franklin Moore was abroad, and odd man used to sneak around to chat and to keep the young wife, sitting alone in the compound, company. He came in the evening when everybody was back to say hello to all and moved on. He was therefore identified as the illiterate man that fathered the second child of the wife of William Moore's son, who was abroad on studies. That unfortunate incident terminated the first relationship of Franklin Moore with a lady. Before this chapter is closed, as we consider this unfortunate incident, I wondered if another method could have been used to keep this young wife from getting pregnant while her husband was abroad studying. What if Esther or Georgina were gay, and while their younger brother was away, they kept their sister-in-law from loneliness and so prevented the intruder from gaining access to their sister-in-law? But oh no, both ladies were holy people and could not have engaged in such nonsense. Esther in particular was stubbornly holy. Gregg stayed with her some years during his high school education, also at Ibadan, and even after he became a man, so he knows her too well. And as for her elder sister Georgina, she was peacefully and quietly holy. None could have done such. But how come it has been said in the West that gayness, HIV, etc., all emanated from Africa? Maybe the whites then had not fully corrupted the African continent with such vices, including cigarettes, drugs, and narcotics.

4. THE GAME OF SOCCER/FOOTBALL

And after graduation from GCI, Moore then moved to Lagos to seek government employment—which was easy then since so few people were educated, unlike now when thousands of Nigerian university graduates cannot find and secure gainful employment. Some even go back for master's programs at home or abroad on scholarship and still return with the employment situation not different from when they left it. It may even be worse! But Moore must have stayed a few years in the Warri-Sapele-Benin axis, doing whatever job he could find but especially playing football or travelling to various cities to watch football matches.

It is at this junction that this author brings in his mother Alice's comment that Daddy Frank would drag her to the faraway city of Benin to watch matches. She was not a bit interested in it. Of course, Dad did not look at her during the match and rarely talked to her and was fully engulfed in the game of soccer that he was watching at the time. I guess her usefulness was her companionship on the way to and from the game of soccer. But she did not mind that role, especially because she knew that many others would give anything to be Franklin Moore's travel companion to and from football matches in foreign cities or even in town!

I am not sure if Mother Alice was the only lady who accompanied Franklin Moore to matches. He had a very serious affair with a lady conventionally described as Moore's original and first wife before my mom came into the picture, and with other mothers of his children, but who, for one reason or another, couldn't give birth to babies at the time. That forced Daddy Frank to succumb to family pressure, I suppose. And that affair died a natural death, but I'm not sure it died in the heart of Aunty Jane, as she was known, as I will later reveal in this book. But after Franklin Moore died in January 1989, though, it can be safely assumed that Aunty Jane was not at the funeral in Lagos, being far away in Benin City! But can this author categorically say that he saw everyone in attendance at that celebration of life?

Daddy Frank continued to play football after his first three sons were born, but this author, the last of the three, did not really witness this because he was the youngest and also partly because his mom took him with her back to Sapele after the age of one but before two, especially with Daddy Frank not in the habit or custom of fighting for child custody during breakups. So again, Alice's son did not experience his daddy playing soccer, but all his life, he saw him watch soccer, not play, where he acted as if the game of soccer contains nearly all the fun and amusement in life.

5. THE ACCOUNTANCY PROFESSION

So Franklin Moore eventually joined the colonial service in Lagos and in no time began to reside in government quarters next to white colonial masters in Ikoyi, an affluent suburb of Lagos away from the Lagos mainland and even Isale Eko, where the indigenous and blacks lived with their king, the oba of Lagos. This profession of accountancy must be greatly esteemed by the whites, or why should Daddy Frank go into it and neglect the possibility or likelihood of taking over Granddad William's profession in local administration in Warri and also anthropology? William Moore wrote the *History of the Itsekiri* that made him a reader associate professor in the University of Sussex, England! Did Franklin Moore begin and end his accounting study at the Government College Ibadan? Certainly not, because after this author's first degree in sociology and anthropology and after entering the MBA program of the University of Lagos with its heavy accounting content, which he did not study prior, searching Daddy Frank's archives brought to open his studentship and internship period with the Society of Commercial Accountants in England and Wales in the late 1950s and early 1960s. The lecture booklets were really useful on the MBA program, though the approach to teaching of the professors of the University of Lagos was American, after Harvard, and not British, as I saw in the books Daddy used to train for accountancy.

The job had another effect on Daddy Moore or, should I say, opened up another chapter in his life that remained with him for the rest of his life. Because he worked as an auditor for many years, auditing government accounts, spending, and receipts throughout the length and breadth of Nigeria, he therefore went on auditing trips to many and all parts of Nigeria—North, East, and the Middle Belt_apart from the South-West, his primary domain—for his primary assignments, where there were federal establishments, sometimes staying there for six months or more—even up to a year—as transfer. But Daddy Frank really knew his onions. This author was once even privileged to work in his private company, the Mawdew Ventures Limited, where he was managing director and chairman on a part-time basis but with a fully equipped staff during his junior college years at the Federal School of Science Lagos, where Daddy Frank's comfort and familiarity with numbers could easily be seen.

By the way, you don't need to work for Daddy Frank in his private company to know he is an accountant par excellence. All you need is to be a son or daughter, living under the same roof with him, where all but one thing he does apart from football is accounting. Unfortunately, or should I say coincidentally, Daddy did not buy into the calculator fever. He used his brain and sometimes paper and pencil. Besides, calculators were not the in things in his time. What this author met in the ministry when he joined in 1971 while working with the Federal Ministry of Finance that was headed by Alhaji Shehu Shagari, the federal commissioner (minister) of finance at the time ever before he became Nigeria's president and commander in chief, was the adding machine. By the way, while still in service, Daddy had always worked in a different department from Gregg Abraham, though all he did, whether good and especially bad, got to his dad wherever he was, sometimes just by a phone call. He never joked with work, either in his civil service job or his private practice businesses that later engulfed all his working hours.

6. FRIENDS AND PROFESSIONAL COLLEAGUES

Daddy Frank worked much and played little, but he did both nonetheless. His professional colleagues were divided into two categories: fellow civil servants who were all blacks like himself and who rarely ever came home to see him. But we children do get to know them in the event of relevancy, like when this author was to join the federal civil service three days after graduation from high school in 1971 and his dad prearranged that he meet Mr. Okwum, a PEO (principal executive officer). Of course, this author was earlier instructed by his dad to write an application for employment, which Daddy read over and made a single correction on (he might mention later) and submitted it on his behalf to the Federal Ministry of Finance. When he came home after writing the last paper of his finals to rest awhile before returning to the boarding house school for end-of-year ceremonies after all students had completed their exams, external and internal.

Daddy's other professional colleagues were all whites (and other) without an exception, and their venue of meeting was sometime, if not most times, in Daddy's study, where these men, also in coats and ties, come to discuss with him. Invariably, they must have been foreigners wanting to do business in Nigeria and seeking a Nigerian partner to have an executive stake in the business, most likely to comply with the federal government registration requirements for Nigerian partnership. Something that probably made Daddy Frank an easy or sure target must have been his area of expertise—accountancy. For I guess had he had been in personnel, for example, he would not have been such a hot cake! Guess Daddy's interactions with these foreign partners made it easy and possible for him to now go into business on his own at retirement or just before retirement. With the litany of companies he formed, it was easy for this present author and his spouse, once when they wanted to go into a buying-and-selling business, to use one of these companies as a springboard.

Daddy Franklin Moore also had friends, but these were much fewer in number than his professional colleagues, and with time, these reduced to three or even two: Mr. Omamogho, also a civil servant with the Nigerian Ports Authority (NPA) until retirement, who lived very closely by, and Uncle Victor Vornick, a hotel owner and businessman who lived in a different city in Lagos but apparently close to Daddy Frank's own city, Surulere, with his wife Anna, who in turn was close to Sisi Funmilayo, one of Daddy Frank's wives who gave him the greatest number of children and one of the few who did not have a prior marriage (catch them young).

Once, after Daddy Frank died and while still in Nigeria, before immigrating to the United States, this author visited Uncle Victor. Not sure how this happened, but I suppose he was driving by and decided to say hello to Daddy's friend, who then sat him down with the announcement that he had a serious matter to discuss with him! Uncle Victor Vornick, in the presence of his wife, Auntie Hannah, wasted no time in telling this narrator the business on hand, and this was what he said: that while FO (for that was what he called him) was still alive, Auntie Peju of Ibadan, the younger sister of Auntie Doyin of Surulere, Lagos, came to Daddy Frank with one of her daughters while she was leaving Nigeria to settle in Great Britain and told the girl "This is where you belong to!" Auntie Peju was a successful married lady with a husband and children in Ibadan, and when relocating one of her daughters to the United Kingdom, she brought her to my family's compound in Ogunlana Drive in Surulere, Lagos, to Daddy Frank and told the girl, "This is where you belong to, that is, this is your father, meaning that his children are your brothers and sisters."

What will you do if you are the one, I ask you, readers? Why did Daddy not tell us, his children, before his exit? But that was not even the thought that came to my mind.

"I will not take this from you, Uncle Victor," I said, "until I verify this piece of information from Auntie Peju herself."

"Fair and good," Uncle and his wife said to me.

But before I took this trip across state lines to Ibadan, the Oyo State capital, to see Auntie Peju, whom I really didn't know but had heard about, this author made a shorter trip within Lagos State to see Auntie Doyin, her elder sister, who knows him well and whom he too knows with a single question.

"Did your younger sister Peji bear a child for my dad?"

"I don't know" was her honest answer, but she added, "I endeavored to give your dad a child myself but was not able!"

And this was a lady that had sons and daughters, all very tall, with her husband, Mr. Amosun, whom I didn't meet or know. By the way, Sisi Funmilayo, the lady that had the greatest number of offspring for Daddy Frank and who also never had a prior marriage, was a junior cousin to Aunties Doyin and Peju and had lived with either sister or at least one of them as a househelp as was common in Nigeria in those days, where poorer extended family members move in to live with richer relations who might be married.

7. AUNTIE JANE

Some years before this author left Nigeria to relocate abroad, about ten and in an ancient city in Nigeria, which he regularly visited for business, in fact he had an office there: Benin City. Yes, he had an office there, but his residence was both in Lagos and Warri, where he also had offices. And everywhere he got to, except when he did not know anybody in the town or city, he normally did not lodge into a hotel. There were two families he lodged with in Benin at different times. One usually lodged him in a small side room, but once, upon arrival with MD, she vacated the master bedroom (which this author never entered or saw the inside from the outside of the door) for MD and him, just like his sister Alero did when he visited her with MD on another occasion in another state capital of Nigeria—Oshogbo of Osun

State. By the way, sister Alero is the first child, and this author is the fifth by the same mom, meaning there are three boys between them. The author later learned online that his hostess number 1 in Benin City has now been dead for about fifteen years, from her colleague at the College of Education somewhere in Edo State Nigeria, Mrs. Yinka Onosode of blessed memory, and may the good Lord bless all her male children without a single daughter and husband too and to receive her gentle soul into Abraham's bosom.

Yinka's residence wasn't this author's only lodging spot in the city of Benin in Edo State. There was another—a pharmacist who was a tenant to an elder lady, an entrepreneur who was probably retired and most likely a pharmacist too. She saw this author come into her compound to lodge briefly and move on but never said a word to him. But once, when MD travelled with him on business, as stated above, he did not usually stay for more than three or four days outside Lagos or Warri. Not sure now if it was on the second or third day, this elderly lady came into the apartment of our hostess, her tenant, and requested that this author and his wife drive after her to an unknown destination to see someone!

They never spoke beyond cordial greetings prior whenever he was in town, and also, maybe she did not even know he was married until MD accompanied him on that trip. If the reader is an African, (s)he would understand a little bit more of the questions that this lady asked the hostess of this author and his wife, MD, for example if they have children and how many. Did this author not say Daddy Frank attended the most prestigious college in the West African region, if not the whole of Africa, and he was the son—the only son—of Sir William Moore, the author of *History of Itsekiri* and a reader at Sussex, England? If this woman, who had never said more to this author other than hello, welcome, goodbye, etc., now, in the very first visit with his wife, called him and said to him and his wife, "Come follow me to another (rich) person—a lady in the ancient city of Benin but of the Itsekiri tribe" Like the hostess and her landlady, one should be ready for action.

So we drove after her, even though I did not know my way through Benin City, until we arrived at a big complex similar to our escort's but maybe a little bigger. As the gate was flung open, we drove in a two-car convoy, and after a brief introduction of less than five minutes, this lady left MD and the author with this woman about her age and drove back to her home.

Both ladies were from Warri, a city of about sixty or so miles from Benin, and they were both Itsekiri ladies. The reader may remember or refer to a book—*The*

History of the Itsekiri by William A. Moore, the father of Franklin Moore, the subject of this book and, by recourse, the grandfather of the present author.

The person to whose house the author and his wife were brought was Auntie Jane. I never saw her but may have seen her picture prior, but again, I am not 100 percent sure about that. But there was rumor that she was a relative of Alice-Tatie, this author's mom, but he never came across her in Lagos, where he was born and was not sure if she ever lived in Lagos but guessed so. But can anyone guess the most important thing about this Auntie Jane, whose house the present writer visited in a convoy after a lady that he thought did not know anything about him but who could have possibly seen him as a suitor of her pharmacist tenant lady, who was also an Itsekiri, took him there? So MD and the writer were guests to this elderly woman who so very lovingly served them dinner and maybe talked a little a bit too. They had some fellowship until he and his and wife drove away and never saw her anymore.

In retrospect, I am very grateful, as I would never have met my august hostess. Yes, I did return to that city, but I certainly did not know my way that night to her house and neither did I take down her address. The discussion was very cordial, and I could see much love and yearning for Daddy Frank in her eyes, but that was it. I was glad I met Aunty Jane and had a firsthand experience of her and all she stood for.

Again, I am not sure why this lady took me to her, but let us make a deduction and guess anthropologically. I suppose after one of my several trips to Benin, this lady must have asked her tenant, Toju, if I was her fiancé and who I really was. And she must had said, "His name is Gregg Moore, and he is a fundamentalist and a pastor." She might have also said that I am married, and she probably also mentioned how she met me through other fundamentalists at Christian fellowship meetings in that city. I was not sure if the landlady asked her tenant how long I had been married or how many children I had in my family and getting answers to all these. It was no wonder that when MD came with me, not knowing if she will ever come again, she wasted no time and escorted us to Aunty Jane's house, did a short introduction, left us there, and drove back home.

Jane, according to history, news, tradition, and gossip was Franklin Moore's official, real, or number 1 wife in a very blissful marriage that ended abruptly without a clash and just because of a different reason entirely. And this single reason had a lot to do with my father as I later came to know him, but this chapter is for Jane, not Frank. As the news went, Jane could not give birth to a baby, and the marriage ended. Who ended it—whether Daddy Franklin or his family—or why the marriage ended was not clear. But it hardly could have been Daddy Franklin, who also had another wife whom I thought was a concubine until another elderly Itsekiri lady in Lagos—not in Benin this time—challenged me and said, "Is it because Paulina did not bear children for your father that you do not regard him as a wife but just a concubine?"

Concubines, whether they bear children or not, generally are sources of conflicts for a bona fide wife or wives and their children at or after the death of the man, with shockers during the reading of the will or last testament of the deceased. Daddy never talked much to his children, but an inquisitive mind such as this author's fortunately or luckily (*though MD is of the opinion that certain men and women, those going to heaven after this life, should not have the latter word in their vocabulary*) did gather information by asking others or merely listening when others talk about themselves or their family. Aunty Esther-Boyowa (meaning "born with joy") told me this story. She too had a delay in childbearing, and as a result of her breakthrough while seeing a gynecologist, she either passed her fertility drugs or her doctor's information to her ex-sister-in-law, who then had her breakthrough in child delivery in her new home after her separation from Daddy Frank, Aunty Esther's younger brother.

By the way, Aunty Jane's son and I met in our university days as undergraduates in the 1970s in Ile-Ife through the National Association of Itsekiri Students. I don't know how I knew he was Aunty Jane's son. Oh, Jane later became known as Mrs. Jane Ogisi. That was how I knew, but I did not disclose this to him, especially since he was not born-again—at least at the time.

Oh, man, in Ife then, yours truly was a member of so many societies, including the Church of England students' group known as the Anglican Youth Fellowship (AYF), because William Moore, whom this author never met alive, lived and died an Anglican. Of course, he was also a member of the BSF, the Baptist Student Fellowship, and two other nondenominational Christian fellowships—the internationally known Student Christian Movement (SCM) and ultra-strong campus fellowship at the time, the ECU, the Evangelical Christian Union. I heard that there is a new group, the student wing of RCCG. That never existed in the '70s but now rules Unife!

So Jane lost her marriage to Frank due to childlessness at the time, but she still became a joyful mother of her children. I was not sure if during that august visit with MD to Aunty Jane in Benin, which I think was in the end of the 1980s, we discussed who my mom was. We should have because children of men with multiple wives are known primarily by the name of their mothers, and these wives are distinguished by their having one child or multiple children, with the lives and history of these children being known in and out, especially that of a lone child in such polygamous homes of wealthy Nigerians. And Jane and Alice were said to be related! Whether they were sisters or cousins, I do not know. But sincerely, I think they are most likely to be cousins, not first or second, but maybe distant cousins.

8. RELATIONSHIP WITH SONS AND DAUGHTERS

Although this work is titled *Franklin Moore: A Nigerian Father* and Franklin Moore is the father of many sons, including the author, Gregg Moore, this Nigerian father had many daughters too. And here, he would venture to expose, declare, or narrate what he thinks this had been, even though he ought not to be the one to write this chapter. Yet he thinks he may be adequately trained to do so, so he ought to go on. In all, this author thinks Franklin Moore had twelve sons and daughters born to him in his lifetime—seven males and five females. Actually, they could be more, but certainly not less. But surprisingly, he thinks (a weak word, really) that Daddy Frank had genuine love for each of his many sons and daughters, though this could be questioned as he never sued for custody or went into battle with any woman that, for one reason or another, refused to surrender his son or daughter to Daddy Frank when that particular lady wanted to move on. These later actions were done by single child spouses, but there was a lady who had at least three children with Daddy Frank who refused to surrender her daughter to Daddy Frank but surrendered her two sons, Irving-Ayiri and Patrick-Oris, until she returned again as Mrs. Moore to take her rightful place as wife, albeit the senior wife. But our concern in this chapter is to discuss or consider the relationship between Daddy Frank and his children, twelve in all as stated somewhere above.

Generally, this author does not remember if any of the girls were whupped in their buttocks, or any other part of their bodies for that matter, like the palm of the hands, etc., for wrongdoings. Even then, when considering the most loved or least loved (though there was no such thing as a least-loved child, or at least Daddy Frank didn't show that). The sons who were born after the first three sons who were born before Nigeria's independence in 1960 never received any whupping! Maybe it was a result of change in the times or by their being children of younger wives or may be of modern times. Also, this author thinks that the older Daddy Frank got, the more he became affectionate to his later-born sons and daughters even though there was no love lost with the older children, of which this writer is one, though it cannot be determined if the older children (in particular, the first three sons) needed to do anything to earn the affection that Daddy Frank showed his later-born sons and, particularly, daughters.

As mentioned earlier in this work, Daddy Frank knew very little, if at all, about his firstborn child—a daughter—because as it happened, he was still a student at the most prestigious college in the West African region, if not the whole of Africa—the Government College Ibadan (GCI). This child died in infancy while she and her mom were living with Daddy Frank's immediate elder sister Esther-Boyowa, who later became Mrs. Esther Foresythe, who worked and retired at the University College Hospital (UCH) in Ibadan.

What relationship did Dad have with his children? A superficial consideration of this might give a misleading impression that he loved his daughters more than his sons, especially since he never whupped any of them, though the older these girls got, there was the possibility of their being scolded and or reprimanded for evil done. One particular example was Evelyn-Baby Moore, who later married Sule Nyelong, a northerner, to become Mrs. Nyelong. I remember clearly in the late 1960s when Evelyn was just beginning high school. She behaved naughtily. I can still remember clearly what really happened, but her game became known to Dad, and he scolded her, I guess even only moderately. God saved her. If she were one of us boys who were older than her, she would not have found it funny at all.

I think that events in the life of a child generally make him or her closer to the parent—for example, should the child be sickly, athletic, a debater, or intelligent at school and may be topping the class. The author fell into one of these categories listed above, which drew Daddy close to him like no other child had the experience or privilege of, yet he does not claim nor does he think he was the favorite child of Daddy Frank. Another factor that possibly determined this was at what age Daddy was when the child was born, meaning, the younger the child, the greater the likelihood that (s)he could be Daddy Frank's most favorable child. As I consider this matter, I remember once when a grandson was brought to him—the firstborn of Patrick-Oris, who, too, is a father now. He was still a toddler then, but as the mother was saluting Daddy Frank, this little baby was jumping and stretching his hands to be lifted by his granddaddy whom I do not even think the baby boy knew well at the time, though certainly, that was not the first time they met. But Sholaye Moore does not qualify at all for the contest, being a grandchild and not a son or daughter.

In considering this, another name comes to mind—Angela-Ogbeyiwa, the only child of her mother and Daddy Frank, who acted exactly like Patrick's firstborn son did, years before any of us got married and, therefore, before Sholaye was born or even conceived. Actually, Patrick-Oris too had not even begun dating Titi, Shola's mom, nor had they met for the very first time. Mrs. Angela Moore-Ajala, like most, if not all, daughters of Franklin Moore, did not live with us at home but lived with her mom outside the Moore compound in Surulere, Lagos. And so once she was brought in, she too jumped up in her mother's arms and wanted to go to her father until the mother eventually released her into her father's arms.

This author is so glad that he personally observed these two incidences, which were over ten years apart. One occurred around 1964 and the other, I think, in 1976! Sincerely, Angela Moore competes very favorably as the most loved child of our dad, but looking back critically now, and for the purpose of analysis, which this book requires, I think she falls short as Daddy Frank's most loved child. I really cannot continue to mention each child because this book is not about any of Franklin Moore's children but about him, and this chapter in particular considers his relationship with his sons and daughters and not the other way round.

There are certain things that the older boys did that Daddy Frank did not do at all and so could not have made him happy at all. For example, Daddy Frank was not a smoker, and at best, he was a social drinker. I'm really not sure if he drank outside his home at all. Even at home, he merely entertained visitors with what they wanted or with his store of wine and beer in the house. This is not to say I have not seen him drunk once or twice in my life. But honestly, he never smoked even a stick of cigarette, got drunk, or used drugs. As a matter of fact, Daddy Frank did not talk to the children about what he did or didn't do or even what he discussed with us individually.

We—or at least I—heard from others about Dad or merely observed or even took part in his activities. One very habit of his—I don't know what chapter this will fit in, but I will be sure to touch on it—about a lady neighbor friend of Dad when I was around seven. Daddy Frank's relationship with me was unique and different. The first major interaction, or should I say meddling, with me was choosing high schools for me in the Common Entrance Examination during my final year in elementary school. Whereas I had really admired Saint Gregory's College in Ikoyi, Lagos, for whatever reasons, especially since it was not really the best in Lagos, for we had (and still have) Igbobi College in

Yaba, Lagos, and King's College, Lagos, but I craved to be a Gregorian. But Dad meddled and chose for me the Government College Ibadan, his alma mater, and Saint Finbarr's College in Yaba, Lagos. Too bad I was not successful in those national exams, but I still had a year more to go since elementary school in Lagos, Nigeria's first capital, was standard and not primary, unlike other schools that existed in all other towns and cities throughout Nigeria, including Ibadan, the nearest regional capital then when there were just three regions. Now, there are thirty-six states. In Lagos, we began with primary 1, then 2 before proceeding to standard 1 to 6. I was in standard 5 when this happened, so I could still go to a higher grade in elementary school, but I did not. I entered high school the very next year!

Firstborn Irving-Ayiri had gotten into Igbobi College in Lagos, and Patrick-Oris was in a Catholic school called Saint Malachy's College, which was very far away from Lagos, in a town called Sapele located between Benin City, the vestige of the Bini Empire of history and the oil-rich city of Warri, where he had performed a never-heard-of feat. He gained a double promotion from form 1 to form 3 for extremely brilliant academic performance. In Nigeria then, high school was for five years. So this January in 1967, as Dad was taking Oris back to school, I went along. But instead of driving away after dropping him, Daddy Frank took me to the principal's office. The principal was Reverend Father Stephens, a huge man just like Goliath in a white gown (cassock). That was all I ever saw him wear. He was from Ireland. How did Dad meddle? He took me for an interview without giving me a hint while we were leaving Lagos for Sapele or even on getting to that town or while waiting to be ushered into the principal's office. So Daddy and I sat opposite the principal. All test questions were orally given and only in two subjects— arithmetic and English (spelling test). The principal quizzed me, and Dad was the scoreboard recorder. Dad immediately shouted *wrong* or *no*—I cannot remember which now—whenever I was wrong. I had never loved mental mathematics, even until now. I preferred it with paper and pencil. But like I said, the impromptu test was all orally given, and as I began to get lost, Daddy would say no, and the tester, the school principal, went to his next question. You will understand and maybe pity my situation if you realize that Daddy Moore was a professional accountant, and what else do they know if not arithmetic or mathematics? The spelling test was not different from and maybe worse than the arithmetic test from my point of view. Words that I knew whose spellings I didn't really know were called out to me to be spelled. And Daddy never wasted time to say *wrong* as the Reverend Father Stephen went on to the next question. At the end of the test, the Reverend Father decided to admit me straight into form 2! You can trust my Dad to again say no. He said I should start from form 1, making me spend five years in high school unlike Patrick-Oris who did it in four, with his double promotion from form 1 to form 3.

One would wonder why an examiner would want to place a candidate who did not do the full entrance exam to start in form 2 instead of 1. Maybe it was because he was from abroad and was used to a four-year curriculum in high school as is the case here in the United States. But he could not change the educational system of a foreign nation. After all, he was brought in by the Vatican as a missionary, not a policy maker. But I also had that same experience last century in the United States when I first arrived. I had gone to the drivers' facility to pick manuals for MD and me to help us prepare for a test for the American drivers' written test for a driver's license. She wasn't ready, so I had to study alone and took the test alone. The test was manual and not automated on a computer in the last century. I'm not sure if it has changed now. Though many people could take the test simultaneously, the marking was done by the proctor after he announced "Pencils up" and marked the scripts individually before each candidate. So during the marking of this written driving test, I saw the proctor marking certain numbers wrong, and I began thinking when I will come again to retake the test after the payment of another testing fee. But surprisingly, the final remark was PASSED after those red markings! He then gave me a certificate to qualify me for the road test when I was ready. You can trust me. I did not fail to ask him how come I passed. Then the proctor told me, "You don't have to score 100 percent to pass." I don't remember if he said that 85 percent or 90 percent is all you need. So my experience with Father Stephen before my meddlesome dad came to mind once again when I found out I can still pass after observing wrong markings in my presence.

It is good to mention that dad am sure did not know how I started grade school a year early, seven years prior, when it was not yet time to be admitted or even enrolled. I was not sure if he knew the drama since he had gone to work so was not able take us (my stepsister and I) to school on the first day of class in the year of Nigeria's independence. This girl, a year older, had been preregistered the previous year without my knowledge. But now that she was beginning school and had a new uniform and other preparations that I could observe, I was not going to stay at home when everybody went to work or school, even though I was five and not six like Gertrude.

Daddy Frank further meddled with me after I completed my five-year high school education when he took me into the office of a university president (called vice chancellor in Nigeria), most likely an alumnus of GCI, to be admitted to medical school without telling me prior to the meeting where we were going. We went only because I had the best result in my school. So Daddy Frank only meddled in his children's lives if his son or daughter creates an enabling environment. Did I mention elsewhere how I started working and earning a salary at the age of sixteen in a federal government ministry (called a department here in America) three days after I graduated from high school, even before the board exam result was released or even marked? After taking my last paper in my final year examinations, I came home to Lagos from Ibadan to later return for the for the end-of- year activities and ceremonies in school in Ibadan. But while at home, Daddy requested I write an application letter for a clerical job at the Federal Ministry of Finance. I wrote it, and he read it and corrected just a word. He told me to change sixteen to eighteen that sixteen-year-olds are not employable by the federal (I guess state) government too!

9. WIVES AND CONCUBINES

Daddy Frank, you must know, was not an American. Instead, he was a British-protected child like his father, my Granddaddy William, or that renowned Nigerian author Chinua Achebe. He was also an African father and, I should add, an African husband too. Though his activities with women are not really different from that of a typical or average American man, he differed essentially in that he did it in the open without fear of possible prosecution, whereas some good people here in America will lie, dissemble, and cover up until the press or some enemies decide to amuse the public, especially if they are running for office or if their enemies want them in jail. What does the Nigerian law say about wives and concubines? I don't really know, even though we were made to say in church during wedding ceremonies, "for better, for worse, stick only to spouse, in sickness and in health, until death do us part." I can write this because I married in church, not in a mosque, court registry, or by tradition. These others are all equally acceptable forms of marriages in Nigeria, where I do not think such vows are required. Oh, why this preamble? All I want to talk about in this chapter is spelled out at the top of this chapter: Wife or Wives and/or Concubines.

But first, we consider a question: who did Daddy Frank love more—his women or his children? This question is asked only because he had more than one woman. In an ideal Christian family, the children come in last and all leave, leaving the original couple with an empty nest. After all, did the Holy Word not say, "The man shall leave his father and his mother and be joined to his wife, shall be one flesh that whatsoever the Lord has joined together let nothing [not even children] put asunder?"

One thing I suppose Daddy Frank dreaded most was a disagreement between a son or daughter with a different mother. He dreaded that more, I suppose, than a fight or quarrel between two wives, which he meticulously made arrangements for so that it never occurred. Another factor that could be considered in this topic of who's first, whether mothers or children, could be gleaned from the African—or is it world—tradition that it is the children and not the wife or wives that continue the lineage. Also in this regard, we also know that the marriage vow lasts as long as both partners are living. So when one partner dies, the other is free to marry another, though there is some fuss about the waiting time the living spouse remains single before remarrying. As a pastor of a church, this author is a foundation member of was asked to resign because the board, or was it the members, felt that his second marriage was too soon after the death of his wife. I had a different reason for opposing the marriage, but that is not for this work.

Really, I do not know the depth of the relationship Daddy Frank had with his women. At best, I can say it varied and depended more on the demeanor of the woman. As I write this, I remember the relationship Daddy Frank had with his only Hausa wife, who undoubtedly was encountered in one of his postings to the northern region of Nigeria for his auditing work as an accountant. This lady rarely talked, and I'm not sure if she even had friends. Maybe not in Lagos since she was based in the north and met Daddy Frank in the north. But she had to return with her husband to Lagos in southern Nigeria after his official duty was over in the north or at least came to visit during her vacation. But this lady had a younger brother who was a student at the

Ahmadu Bello University (ABU) in Zaria, whom daddy adopted as son and who came to live with us more often than his sister while he was an undergraduate in the university. Daddy Moore's disconnection with his women most likely could have been a result of the gap in educational attainment between him and these women. Mommy Alice, for example, went to high school after I was born and had graduated from high school, and that, of course, was in London, United Kingdom, a far more literate society than Nigeria, where she later took as her home. Not to be forgotten was a story she told me of her dread while in the examination hall for the London General Certificate of Education (GCE) Ordinary Level! Another mistaken notion, of course, was or still is that a woman's primary role is to bear children. I may be wrong, but I do think that Daddy Frank, while he was still alive, had he been interviewed by reporters to choose whom he loved more—children or wives—would have chosen children.

Again, this section of the book is on wives and concubines. Without any contest whatsoever, Jane is known by all and sundry as Daddy Frank's no. 1 wife even though she did not have any issue in the marriage and later remarried with multiple conceptions, making her a joyous mother in a second marriage with medical referral assistance provided by Aunty Esther-Bayowa,

Daddy Frank's immediate elder sister. We also have talked about the young lady who was first to bear a child for Daddy Frank in the early the 1930s while he was still a student at the most prestigious college, the Government College Ibadan, whose child died in infancy and because of some social accident, could not be retained with her in-laws while Daddy Frank was still in college and had to be let off.

It appeared that Daddy Frank did not go out of his way to look for female partners. They just fell into his normal pathway in life like the nurse that later became his wife. According to his eldest sister, Georgina-Omajurun, they met when he was in the hospital ward as an inpatient. She must have taken special care of him or some spark just ignited between them so that after his discharge from the hospital, the relationship continued. She left her real husband for Daddy Frank. Other places where Daddy Frank met partners were in the federal government ministries (departments) where he worked. And as a result of his profession, he never stayed in a ministry for long and did not stay until retirement. The two wives he got there were Theresa and Paulina, incidentally both secretaries and Igbo speaking. Theresa had a daughter, and Paulina had no issue for him or for any other man. The latter married him, and they remained married until his death. As for the former, she told this writer that Daddy Frank was very nice and that she loved him, but she had to end the marriage for her peace of mind because of the other women in his life. For a long time, she too had no child. It was not clear if, after she moved out, she discovered she was pregnant (the popular version) or as I write this now, on discovering she was pregnant and not to lose the baby (she must have had miscarriages in the past), she moved out to rent her own apartment with two daughters she brought in from a previous marriage. And so Angela-Ogbeyiwa, whom I had mentioned somewhere in this work to possibly be the best loved child, was born.

It cannot be really explained why Daddy Frank was more interested in women that had married or are married than single, unmarried ladies. But a possible reason could be the fate he suffered when another man came after the mother of his very first daughter while he was away in college in faraway Ibadan, in the home of his elder sister, who too was educated like him and had to go for a white-collar job, leaving her sister-in-law alone at home with a baby!

But one thing that was clear was that these women preferred him to their current or ex-husbands. There was Aunty Doyin in Lagos. She was very rich, with landed properties and children of her own from a present or previous marriage, and she loved Daddy Frank far more.

Actually, one of my elder brothers, Irving-Ayiri, used to frequent her home as *omo oko* (a husband's child). I was not sure if Patrick-Oris did too, but it is very likely. Aunty Doyin had a younger sister in Ibadan who was also married with children in her matrimonial home. And news was rife that both Doyin and Peju were concubines of Daddy Frank. And because we lived in Lagos, I knew Aunty Doyin very well but only heard about Aunty Peju, a businesswoman in Ibadan. A supposition is that she must have been in Lagos before her marriage that took her to Ibadan, or how else could Daddy Frank have known her? There was a third—Sisi Funmilayo—who had the greatest number of children with Daddy Frank—three boys and one girl—a cousin to Doyin and Peju, who must have been adopted by elder sister Doyin and living with them when Daddy Frank met her. In chapter 6, I narrated a story I heard through his best friend, Uncle Victor Vornick, about my experience and discovery after Daddy Frank died. All these women were present during the wake of his funeral, each having separate canopies and sections.

10. Relationship with William Moore, His dad, Even in the Afterlife

Very unfortunately, none of us children were alive in the lifetime of Granddaddy William. This was unlike what happened a generation prior, for as Aunty Esther-Boyowa would say, she saw her Grandfather Akenbo (Akinbo), who married into the Itsekiri royalty, and could mention some of his mannerisms and words. Much more, however, is learned from the oral history and tradition as discussed by the Itsekiri people and by scholars from the neighboring tribes of the Itsekiri, notably the Urhobo scholars, with Professor Obaro Ikheme of the University of Ibadan as a key scholar. But much more could be learned and expanded about Granddaddy William from his work, *History of Itsekiri*, even though little about him was said in that work.

GREGG MOORE

I think Daddy Frank and his two elder sisters were the best to talk to about their dad, including Granny Akpero, wife of William Moore, who lived over thirty years after the death of her husband. But unfortunately, she never told this author anything about her husband or about anything whatsoever, not even about herself or any of her children or even bedtime stories. She just concentrated on the welfare of this third grandson of hers—this author. Also, this author was not yet trained then in the act of writing and research to have seized upon the golden opportunity that he had with his grandmother, who stayed with him more than any of his siblings or even Daddy Frank, at least after he was born. Dad only came into her room once in a while to get counsel or ask how she was doing and also for the name of a newborn child. It appeared to this writer though that Daddy Frank viewed his father, Granddaddy William, as probably more than a man!

Another determinant of how Daddy Frank led his life could be derived from how he observed Granddaddy William lived—the latter's philosophy about family, women, and life vis-à-vis work. It appeared Daddy William did not place a high value on a large family to do farmwork for him as he also did not do farmwork but was a man of the pen. And even if he needed work done in his farms, which were many and very expansive, there were workers he owned as a result of the administrative position he held - which position was the go-between his people and the whites. So his family was small, with only three kids—two girls first and then a boy. This author has heard in modern times, while gathering materials for this work from very reliable quarters, that he probably had other children from outside his marriage. But if this were true, they were not as educated as the children of housewife Granny Akpero, and so the idea of two names, a first name and a surname, did not arise if indeed there were children born to William Moore outside wedlock. How did Granddad take it when his first child was a girl? Who knows, but when the secondborn arrived, Esther, she too was a girl. Could he have been crossed with his wedded wife for conceiving and giving birth to two girls in a row? However, Daddy Frank came along last. After giving birth to him, Granny Akpero did not bear anymore! Was William then satisfied that he now had a son, or was the burden and the responsibility of the work on his shoulders too much that he cared less about women, family, and children?

This brings us full circle to Daddy Frank's own attitude toward women, family, and children, for he had them in abundance far more than his father—our grandfather—or his grandfather—our great grandfather. For while the former had only two daughters, he had more than double the number of daughters. And as for sons, whereas Granddaddy William had only one son, Daddy Frank had more. For instance, this author was his third son. And after him were far more sons born to him like Daniel (Joseph) Michael-Muyiwa, Gbubemi-Feyi, Niyi-Aju, etc. These are not mentioned, however, in order of birth.

While on the MBA program of the University of Lagos, Daddy once came to visit his son in his room, which was so very unusual, a thing he did not do when Gregg Sr. was in high school, junior college or at the University of Ife during his bachelor's degree years. But he did come for his graduation ceremony at Ife, or more appropriately, the whole family attended the University of Ife graduation ceremony since Gregg Sr. was no longer on the campus or in the university town of ancient Ile-Ife but was on the National Youth Service in faraway Enugu State.

Once, when Daddy Frank visited this author at the Fagunwa (postgraduate) Hall of the University of Lagos, he told him what he never did and talked about his father, William, and what he achieved in life—what people thought about him, said about him, and how he was revered and honored. This entire scenario Daddy Frank viewed as a positive correlation of his son being on the university of Lagos MBA program, which was a glimpse and a positive resemblance of what Granddaddy was and what he achieved in life! It became clearer to this author, therefore, why on every New Year's Day, Daddy Frank sacrificed to his father and invited many to feasting and celebration, which he never failed to do annually. Did I say he invited? The people knew there was celebration on the first day of the new year in Franklin Moore's quarters and so didn't need to be invited to be in attendance. And because it was an all-day celebration, many people resorted thither after attending to other engagements they have for that public holiday or maybe first show up at the Moore's before going elsewhere. But this celebration was an all-day affair from morning till dusk with visitors coming and going and others remaining all day, dining and dancing.

Daddy Frank, must have seen the burden placed on him to succeed in life because of the achievement of his grandfather and how the baton was very successfully handed over to his father, who indeed proved himself a very worthy successor of his father, Granddaddy Akinbo (Akenbo). And incidentally, both Akinbo and William-Apieyi had only a son each. Daddy Frank, however, had at least six sons! He was really worried that he may not raise a successor who will continue the legacy and tradition of Akinbo, William, and Franklin in this modern age when it appears that for so many diverse reasons, continuing the family tradition or legacy did not seem to feel binding or appealing to the new generation.

11. His Religion

Daddy Frank took the fourth commandment that says "Remember the Sabbath day to keep it holy" very, very seriously. Though I cannot remember the church life or religion of my family at ages zero to three, shortly after that, I do remember very, very distinctly. Elsewhere, I mentioned that Daddy Frank worships—or is it adores—his father, Granddaddy William. Once every year on New Year's Day, so many natives came around to partake in this annual celebration of feasting and dancing plus some prayers he made to his father, which was the highlight of that celebration, though it was not mandatory for any to be present at the place and time of the prayer. I think the purpose of the crowd going there was the free drinks and food plus the dancing and good time and maybe meeting people one might not have seen for a long time or just meeting someone for some personal reasons, using Franklin Moore's event as a rendezvous. You, as a guest, did not need to go say hi to the celebrant—Daddy Frank—neither was there a gate fee or gateman on that day to allow some in and prevent others from gaining entry. But that was about everything for Daddy never discussed it or mentioned it until exactly another year after. He didn't mention it then too, but that ball just started to roll. Also his outside auditing tours for the federal government never occurred during this time, for every arm of government is on recess just before Christmas until the second of January at the earliest or even third or fourth if this fell on, say, Thursday or Friday.

But Daddy Frank gave at least fifty-two days to the God of Israel annually. He never missed church. He went to the First Baptist Church Lagos at the intersection of Broad and Joseph Streets, and his seat was never taken by another. I shall return to that point soon. He went to church with his entire household—wife, children, and stepchildren, with the exception of his sick mom and the household servants, who never left home except on errands. Surprisingly, even staunch Roman Catholic wives gave up their devotion to the Virgin Mary to go with Daddy Frank to worship in the American Baptist way until, for whatever reason, the marriage fell apart and they go and pick up their rosaries once again. In saying this, I have a particular stepmother in mind— Aunty Theresa. But I will return to this shortly. As we were growing up—us first three boys—the Baptist liturgy consisted of a handful of observations—three or four at the most. But of course, a few others were for specialized people like the one that Ivynn-Ayiri belonged to, which I never knew the time they met for practice, I mean, at the First Baptist Church Lagos and not the New Estate Baptist Church, which Ivynn-Ayiri did not go to with Patrick-Oris and this author since he had left for the boarding house at Igbobi College in Yaba, Lagos, when New Estate began as a preaching station and Daddy Frank moved us there, which most likely was the beginning of his exit from church. Yes, the regular liturgy were the following: the Sunday morning worship service, the Sunday school of for all ages before, and the midweek prayer meeting, which we never went to since Daddy did not take us in his car as he does on Sunday mornings, and I don't think he went too. The meeting firstborn Ivynn-Ayiri attended was the choir practices, which were for **selected people who not only dress differently from the entire church but in unity.** They also sat in a specialized position, facing the whole congregation for all to see them, and sang some songs no one else could sing along to, but they sang along with the congregation any song the congregation sang. I was not sure if Daddy Frank attended church business meetings, but I guess he did since his profession, talents, and endowments were called for and will be needed in such church meetings to thrash out certain matters.

One aspect of the church that was really remarkable and memorable to me was the Sunday school, which was by age grades. We all sat in the main church auditorium, where a hymn or two were sung and an adult male came forward to give a short speech while referring to a book. After that, we children were sent out of the main church to different classrooms in the school—the Ade-Oshodi Memorial Baptist School, a story building adjoining the church to the school Iynn-Ayiri attends Monday through Friday. I think the only time he was not in the Baptist mission compound was on Saturdays. As for Patrick-Oris, he attended Saint David's School of the Church of England, the Anglican Church, while I wasn't in school yet, all the time we were living in Ikoyi in Lagos Island. After the Sunday school, we continued in classroom church or extended Sunday school, with no choir or pulpit or pastor and his special sermons and final invitations every Sunday. These children's classes had more than one teacher, who took turns to be away from us to attend the main (adult) church! This made us—or should I say me—a lot curious, so I always ran to the big church after we were dismissed to look for Daddy Frank, even though I knew where the car was parked on our arrival. Of course, there were policemen at the various entrances of the church (we later discovered they were called ushers), and as they were caught up in something—or even if they were vigilant—we children sneaked through them and went in, looking for our parents. As for Daddy Frank, it was so easy to locate him because he sat on the same seat Sunday after Sunday, but I guess he must have sat some pews to the left or right on one of two rows. And when he saw me looking for him, even though he never spoke a word, the look on his face would tell you what will come after in the car before getting home. Nonetheless, I didn't think I stopped this until we second and third born were transferred to nearby New Estate Baptist Church to home, whose whole service from start to finish was in the classrooms of the Municipal Primary School on Itire Road near Randle Avenue in New Lagos, later known as Surulere.

Yes, Daddy Frank went alone or with a wife to the First Baptist Church Lagos after he bought his first home in Lagos in 1959 as we moved away from government quarters on Lugard Avenue in Ikoyi, Lagos, where some neighbors were whites with dogs, to Ogunlana Drive in Surulere, where all neighbors were black and mainly from the east, west, and midwest, that is, Igbos, Efiks, Ijaws, Yorubas, Binis, Itsekiris, Urhobos, etc. I did not really know when Daddy Frank dropped out of church as we two, Patrick-Oris and I, one after the other, left home for the boarding house, unlike Iynn-Ayiri, who went to Igbobi College, a mission school jointly owned by the Methodist mission and the Church of England in Yaba, Lagos, and we next two to faraway Sapele, a town midway between Benin City and Warri to Saint Malachy's College. One thing about Daddy Frank's religion and commitment to the Baptist faith was how he took it when I announced to him sometime in 1968 that I had been baptized as a Catholic and have taken the saint name Gregory! The additional Christian name did not disturb him since he too has an English name—Franklin. I was not sure if the Baptists do the saint thing like the Roman Catholics, but I was baptized into another religion or denomination when all he wanted me to do when he sent me there was to gain education and not change denomination. I continued with the Catholic Church even after being born again in another mission school in Ibadan, Nigeria—the Mount Olivet—in 1970 until junior college before returning to New Estate Baptist Church in Surulere in 1973, which now has moved away from a school building to its permanent site on Adisa Bashua Street, also in Surulere in Lagos State.

Another dimension to Daddy Frank's faith could be gleaned from his reaction to my announcement in 1974 that I would not be studying medicine anymore, for God, I said, had called me to full-time ministry to become a pastor! Incidentally, my call to the ministry did not take place in the Baptist setting but in the Church of England setting at the wake-keeping service of his brother-in-law, Sidney Olayinke Foresythe, husband of Aunty Esther Boyowa Foresythe, née Moore. It was a wake-keeping service, not an evangelist service or a call to the ministry service. But I heard God clearly saying to me, "This is my will for your life," while listening to the Anglican clergy talk about the hope of the dead in Christ. By the way, this was two years before I met MD. And though I applied to the Nigerian Baptist Theological Seminary in Ogbomosho, an overseas campus of the Southern Baptist Theological Seminary in Louisville, Kentucky, and gained admission to come in for a four-year degree program in theology, Daddy Frank, an accountant whose dad Granddaddy William was an anthropologist and historian, said his son would not be a church pastor despite the fact that I told him God asked me to be a preacher. Instead, he gave an alternate career to this author—law—if he would not study medicine anymore, even though he was not part of his third-born son's decision to read medicine in the first place! Was Daddy Franklin Moore tough, I ask? Yes, he was, though he was very reasonable too. He attended the graduation for my first degree even though I didn't read law for my first degree with my medicine prerequisite and instead chose to read a course I just read about while reading the autobiography of Dr. Billy Graham. He studied anthropology at Wheaton College in Illinois, USA. Yes, Daddy was not pleased, yet he financed the degree program.

He later was led by a wife or wives to some denomination that the Nigerian Evangelicals did not consider Christian. Miraculously, this author challenged him to return to the Baptist Church, which he did and even showed him the proof of his return. The reader, especially the American reader, may not appreciate what was just stated above—how a son, a fry, challenged his father to return to church and the latter obeyed and positively responded. When this son later gave him a Bible, this was what he wrote in the Bible: "Presented to me by my son, the Reverend Gregg Onoghoete Moore." He then signed it, and it is now being used by MD. Regrettably though, Daniel, whom I choose to call Joseph (favorite of our father), immediately picked it up and took possession of it after

Daddy Frank's death. But I got it from him because I was older (in the first three), which this author now sincerely regrets. This author did not have a family altar, where fathers, mothers, and children gather together to read the Bible and pray together before setting out for the day. Instead, we children did our house chores and got ready to enter the car when Daddy Frank was out to enter the car to drive or be driven to work. Actually, this author only had that luxury when it rained overnight and was taken to school, which was not more than a thirty-five-minute walk from home unlike numbers 1 and 2 who attended school in the Lagos Island, where the federal government departments (ministries) were located and where Daddy Frank worked. I had thought that the Bible was read only in church on Sundays until in the eleventh grade in high school (form 4) when some guys, two, really—Dr. Clement Ojeh and his partner, **Dr. Wilson Badejo**—both undergraduates then from the London University College in Ibadan Nigeria, then known as the University of Ibadan, which took away the glory from the Government College Ibadan (GCI)— came one Sunday afternoon in May and told us about a new and better way to relate to God, which included reading the Bible every day, praying, etc., after first becoming born again. One of the two was able to preach to the entire boarding house of students because the ecclesiastical preacher arrived late. His arrival made the two university undergraduates run away from the pulpit area, but he asked them to continue and also encouraged the boarding house students to listen to them and take their sermons seriously.

12. MY ASSESSMENT OF FRANKLIN MOORE IN LIFE

Sincerely or seriously, I think this book is complete, but why is there a twelfth chapter? **My narration** is over because this author does not think he is qualified to evaluate his father. In the Moore lineage, no son or daughter is qualified to evaluate his or her father. Did you not read a while ago how Daddy Frank annually celebrated his father, our Granddaddy William? He once told me about his father as if he were more than life while he was sitting on my bed at the Fagunwa (postgraduate) Hall of the University of Lagos while undergoing my first master's degree program—an MBA. He almost was lamenting a downturn in the family tree and maybe saw a ray of hope in my getting on the MBA program after shunning medicine and even law, his alternative for me. I actually heard later outside that an MBA was a shortcut to management positions in Nigeria and, I guess, in the whole world. Nigeria certainly cannot be different from the rest of the world when it comes to climbing the corporate ladder. As for the relationship between Granddaddy William and Great-Granddaddy Akinbo (Akenbo), Granddaddy William was just a kid despite all his achievements, and Great-Granddaddy Akenbo made it all happen for Granddad William, he being married to a princess and being the son-in-law of a monarch.

The purpose of this chapter is to evaluate my dad—I'm sorry—*our* dad.) I do not think I am the most loved of the children, though in some ways, chance, it may be said, made it look so. But Daniel, whose real name should be Joseph Omatseyin, just like the eleventh son of Jacob (Israel), is a lot like him in all good and great qualities and maybe some bad ones, if you will say. But I don't think Daddy Frank had any bad qualities. By the way, Daniel-Omatseyin did not play football like Daddy. It was Patrick-Oris who did. But Daddy Frank loved football singularly against all other sports, that no other sport came second. Daddy Frank's kids were not privileged like him and his sibling to meet their grandfather while he was still alive. As for his mom, officially called Madam Akpero Moore (I wonder why she was not just Mrs. Akpero Moore. To us all, she was Big Mama—Mama Kporo), whom many of his children met alive, she Daddy Frank revered a lot. Daddy Frank did not name a single child until after 1968, when his mom died! Whenever a child was born on the morning of the eighth day, Daddy Frank did something he always did when a new child is born and came to his mother's room, which I shared with her and inherited after 1968, to get the name(s) of the new child. So even though I do not know how I or Orioye or Ayiri was named, I know the process could not be different. Maybe I followed the pattern to name our only son, G. M. Oritsemi, after Daddy Frank. But MD challenged her exclusion from the naming process before the birth certificate was issued and said that it should be G. M. Ayomikun, which I had to concur to. After all, she was from another unique family, with its history only marrying into William Moore's family, son of Akenbo and father to Daddy Frank Oritsemi, with its distinct tradition and culture.

All of Daddy Frank's women adored him, though Mommy Alice has not or did not speak so glowingly of him to this author. She does not speak glowingly of men in general. But equally, she also did not say anything bad about him to me or in my presence. I almost could have said maybe she told her mom, my maternal grandmother, but it is extremely doubtful and may be impossible. One thing Mommy Alice stressed to me was that he was so caught up with football and would drag her to matches, whether in Sapele, Benin, Lagos, or anywhere else, and didn't know that she wasn't hooked to soccer like him. I guess she was happy though to be the one going to matches with him, a role that other ladies would have been eager to play. I guess Mommy Alice did not understand or share the joy of shouting on the football field when a team wins or the depression of some other fans of the team that loses. Auntie Theresa told me she left not because of being hurt by her ex-husband, Daddy Frank, but only because of the other women in his life. What logic! I really wonder how Americans will take that argument, even though they would still love her because she left and did not stay. So many people criticized Hillary Clinton, the almost first lady president of America for not leaving her husband Bill.

Somewhere in this book, I calculated Daddy Frank's children to be twelve, almost like Israel, but they could be much more or at least a little bit more. Daddy Frank had intimate female friends who were happily married. And some could be sisters to each other. Earlier, somewhere in this book, I insinuated that Alice and Jane are related, but I do not know how close. But there were two sisters, Doyin and Peju, both happily married with children, who I heard or knew were Daddy Frank's concubines. I know Doyin very personally because she was in Lagos, where we all were, but her sister Peju settled in Ibadan as a big-time entrepreneur. I sincerely never met her until Daddy Frank's death and, of course, until after marriage, which preceded his death. I think I already narrated this elsewhere in this work. After Daddy Frank's death, his friend Uncle Victor Vornick, in the presence of his wife, Anna, told me about a child, a daughter of my dad and told me who the mother is! He said he was telling me because I am a reverend, knowing fully well that I am neither the no. 1 son nor no. 2, and then charged me with the responsibility, or was it that he considered it that I have the ability or the know-how, to bring this lost daughter into the family. This is akin, though in an opposite but positive way, to how King David charged his successor and son to take down Army Commander Joab, his nephew and successor's first cousin and another man, Shemei, a kinsman of Israel's first monarch, Saul, to whom David said, "Do not make his hoar hair to go to the grave in peace" (1 Kings 2:6, 9).[4]

The first thing I did was to narrate the whole story to MD. And next, I went to Auntie Doyin's house on Ibidun Street in Surulere, Lagos, to authenticate the report I just received from Uncle Victor and inquired if her sister Peju had a child with Daddy Frank. She said she honestly didn't know and added that she did all she could to have children with Daddy Frank but couldn't, and this is remarkable because she was not barren, for she had sons and daughters with her husband, Mr. Amosun. Next, together with MD, we traveled to the ancient city of Ibadan to search out Auntie Peju. We guessed that she lived in Challenge Layout in Ibadan. The trip was fruitless, so MD and I returned home to Lagos State. But sometime later, I decided to go, alone this time, since I didn't know if MD will once again want to go out on a wild-goose chase. I did not really know what went on in her mind, whether or not what I was doing meant anything to her, coming out from a family of one man and one woman without any outside encroachment—I almost said outside concubine.

This time around though, the search in Challenge, Ibadan, began as it did previously, but luck, some would say, shined on me. I got the exact description of the mansion from the first inquiry I made on the street in the suburban village of Challenge, and on ringing the bell, an attendant came, asked who I wanted, let me in, led me to the sitting room, and went to announce my presence. All this happened before I relocated and changed my nationality. I wish to say that my journey was extremely successful, but the reader is the judge.

The mistress of the house came down and sat not too far away from me, without any real emotion as I began to speak. I must have started by mentioning that I am Daddy Frank's third son. I cannot remember exactly now, but I got to the reason why I came and maybe also mentioned that I once came with my wife, but we couldn't find her and so returned to Lagos.

I eventually mentioned my discussion with Uncle Victor. She did not say "Who is Victor Vornick?" She did not even ask me to identify myself, especially since Daddy Frank was light-skinned, and I am maybe as black as a charcoal, as many of Daddy Frank's children are (about 65 percent).

"Did you have a daughter with my dad and brought her home to Ogunlana Drive in Surulere, Lagos?" I had asked her. All she said was "I did not get a cent [kobo] from any man to train any of my children." I guess she said I should be served, but I am not sure what it was that was served or even if I tasted any food there before the best happened. Guess what? This lost sister of mine, who is a British resident or citizen and who was unknown to me was in Nigeria at the time with her mom in Ibadan. But she was out at the time I was at their home! Then the bell rang. *Oh, another visitor might be coming in,* I thought. Somebody went out to open the gate, and she came in. She was almost a carbon copy of another daughter of Daddy Frank from a different mom who resembles him the most. I was introduced to her, and we bonded. I got her contact number in London and told her I would be leaving shortly to the United States to North Kenilworth Avenue in Oak Park in the state of Illinois, our temporary stop before we settled down on our own. I later went back to Uncle Victor and Anna Vornick. I really wanted to talk only to Victor, but Anna always sat beside him. I never addressed her when talking to Uncle apart from the initial greetings. But this time, she spoke as I was narrating the outcome of my two fact-finding tours to Ibadan. I then told the elderly couple that upon confronting Aunty Peju about my knowledge of the news of her visit to our home in Lagos with a daughter to see my dad, which I got from Uncle Victor, I asked her to concur or refute my findings. Her answer was "I do not get money from a man to train any of my children."

Then Aunty Anna responded, "You are a child. You don't need any more proof, and after all, she did not deny your allegation." She did not even add "After all, you also saw your sister."

As an exhibit, here is the letter Uncle Victor wrote to me here in the United States, mentioning Peju's daughter, on emigration abroad.

But before leaving Nigeria, I announced to the Franklin Moore family the news of a lost sibling now found, which did not cause a small stir but a big one, especially from Evelyn-Tosanwunmi, who challenged me that I was attempting to get my mother's daughter to take her position as the eldest daughter of Daddy Frank.

Daddy Frank was also very concerned about the education of his children, knowing the value of education. This writer used to say it was one of the three things he realized the Nigerian society esteemed above all, the other two being age and money. But writing now, he can see that he learned not from Nigeria per se, but from the lineage of Moore through which yours truly accidentally came into this planet Earth. I remembered once in junior college. It was before the exact time for me to sign up for the University of London Advanced Level General Certificate of Education, an examination that lasts for at least one week. I wanted to take this exam externally and choose a center outside Lagos State in faraway Ibadan. Now where will I stay? But Daddy Frank had already arranged that I would stay in one of the high-rising flats of the GRA in Ibadan, in the home of a bank executive of the Central Bank of Nigeria in Ibadan, who either was not yet married or that his wife was abroad at the time. So I had this residence to myself, keys and all, even though the man came in to sleep at night. We left home at different times of the day. He only took me in his car when I had a morning paper. Up dad! He would do anything for any of his children to climb the academic ladder!

There is one more thing this author wishes to say, which is not much of an incident, but he remembers it as if it happened yesterday. He was not even ten years old at the time—maybe eight or nine. Daddy Frank's women loved him so much, no matter who they were and whatever their state in life was. But somehow, he never was interested in younger girls, the extreme of which would have made him a pedophile had he been domiciled in the United States and so be contravening the law. He was interested in women who most likely are established in life like him and who most likely would tell no one, I suppose, or would not share the secret with anyone. At the time, I most likely was eight, maybe not nine or even seven, and I say this for different reasons. Daddy Frank had given me a handwritten note and instructed me to whom I should give it in the neighborhood. I am not sure what day of the week it was, but it could not have been Sunday because on Sundays, we go to church. Neither could it have been Monday through Friday since, as I said elsewhere in this work, during those days, all that we did was prepare and get out of the house, even without having a morning devotion, so as to beat the traffic. I suspect it was on a Saturday, but it could have been during the period of Daddy Frank's annual leave, and so he was at home in the morning when most people were not. This lady I was to give Daddy's note to was a housewife and had children as old as Daddy Frank's first son or maybe even older. She was beautiful, serene, and respectable. Why I did not open the letter and read it, I don't know. I would have included the content here now. I also don't know why I did not take the note to my playmate to read together, but I can conjecture that I was not in any gang, and neither did I have a particular friend in the neighborhood who was my special friend. And when your dad sends you on errand in those days (I doubt if it has changed), woe betide you if you do not attend to it with urgency, immediacy, and alacrity. So I got into this house, a small boy, made my way to this woman, and said, "My dad said I should give you this note."

I am not sure if I waited for her to read so as to get a written reply back to Daddy Frank, but I must have because after reading, she was full of smiles and said to me, "Tell him he has a lot of paper (writing materials)! Of course, I dare not return such a message to my dad. But if she had written something, I would gladly have returned with her note back to daddy Frank, also without being curious about its content. Looking back while writing this now, I tried to find a reason why Dad did this—not why he was so lucky with these women, but why he did it at all. Certainly, he was not the richest around for someone to say they all wanted his money or even if any of them wanted his money. I think we were all around the same family income bracket, though Daddy Frank chose to own three to four cars at a time, which was not the custom at that time, and to get a driver for each car. What I discovered must have affected him was a story told to me by Aunty Esther, Dad's immediate elder sister, who I am sure did not divulge the story to any other of my siblings, so I most likely would be the only one who knows this story about the reason for Daddy Frank's actions in this aspect of his life. She told me about a man who came and lured the mother of his first child into sex while he was away in Government College Ibadan (GCI) and his sister was away at work. Did I say Daddy's first child died, and the young mother became pregnant without Aunty Esther Foresythe, a.k.a. Mama Yemi knowing? Yes. It was while Daddy Frank was away in college. It was even a neighbor who asked her, "Do you not see your brother's wife is pregnant?" And she regretfully told me this over fifty years later. She had not once been pregnant when this occurred and so did not know the signs of pregnancy. Her only son is Ibiyemi, my first cousin, also in his sixties and now a father and grandfather. Or could he be a great-grandfather too? I don't think so.

There is something else I wish to touch on in the life of Daddy Frank—how he treated people in need even when they were not related to him by blood. But first, let's close the section above. What does God think about this? In response, we may consider the matter of David versus Uriah, Bathsheba, et al. We all know how it all went, but what did God say to David after it all?

> ***And I gave thee thy master's house, and thy master's*** wives into thy bosom, and gave thee the house of Israel and of Judah; and if *that had been* too little, I would moreover have given unto thee such and such things.9 Wherefore hast thou despised the commandment of the Lord, to do evil in his sight? thou hast killed Uriah the Hittite with the sword, and hast taken his wife *to be* thy wife, and hast slain him with the sword of the children of Ammon. (2 Sam 12:8)

God said to David, "I could have given you more wives[3] but why did you kill Uriah?"

Daddy Frank loved and was kind to people, even those not related to him by blood. Nigeria had a bloody civil war around 1967, when all Igbos left all regions of Nigeria and headed home to the southeast to create the Republic of Biafra. In our neighborhood in Surulere, Lagos, families loaded their household items and moved en masse back home to Eastern Nigeria, as it was then called. This was in 1966. But the war eventually ended, and those who left started retracing their steps and started coming back. In Lagos, where Daddy Frank lived and worked, he had so many people under him, mostly southerners. So after the war, his home became a meeting place for Ibo refugees, those who had worked under Daddy Frank in the various federal ministries (departments). They came, mainly wanting to be rehired into the federal service! But Daddy Frank was never in Human Resources or Personnel but was in Accounting and Finance, yet it was to him that all these former public servants came. Of course, he couldn't absolve all those who left their job to start a new country that was actually started but was dissolved by a man named Gowon, Yakubu, whose name was given the meaning "Go On with One Nigeria" and who later rose to be an army general. There was a day when a young man came to our home. This was after 1971, when I had completed high school and was then a salary earner.

So when I told him Daddy was not in, he said that that was all right and that it was me he came to see, not my dad. From what I got from him, Daddy had really tried for him, but he was still in need. And because I was a salary earner, he wondered if there was something I too can chip in for his sustenance. I was not really seventeen yet. Actually, he told me about a vow he made on New Year's Day, and this was about two years before God called me into full-time ministry at the wake-keeping service of the late Sydney Olayinka Foresythe, the father of my cousin Ibiyemi Foresythe. This young man had said to himself—or was it to God—that if things didn't improve, he was going to join the Roman Catholic priesthood. I suppose this was because it was a secure livelihood and would exempt him from paying taxes. On that day, I went into my safe. I think I acted on behalf of Daddy Frank and shared with his visitor, in his absence, my pounds and shillings.

Another thing about Daddy Frank, which I surprisingly have not mentioned until now, is that he was soft-spoken and never ever raised his voice while talking to anybody, no matter the subject of conversation. Although I cannot say the same for what happens on the football field, where I suppose we hear jubilant screams intermittently during a game and a final shout at the end by the supporters of the winning team. I will not be surprised though if his roaring was soft compared to that of anyone in the audience. He had his soccer days and was now a spectator. This does not mean he did not address situations squarely. Though often, instead of speaking, he just kept silent. Do not think he ever used abusive words against anyone unlike some or most of his children—Daniel excluded but including this present author. Have you ever heard of the word *scallywag*? Actually, I never knew its true spelling until now, and I had used it whenever I was angry, especially with someone who asks me what it means. I didn't know at all. I only heard it on the streets of Lagos in my preteens. In fact, I spelt *scallywag* wrongly before the computer I was on corrected it. This was growing up in Lagos, which Daddy Frank did not have the luxury of experiencing. Of course, he came to Lagos after his life in Ibadan, the most primitive area of Nigeria, at least when compared to Lagos. But did I say life in Ibadan? The government college was in the outskirt of Ibadan then before the city grew up to catch up with it and spread farther outward. Yet GCI was not Ibadan though in Ibadan with all those white students and teachers! Only the gardeners and cooks and gatemen and household servants must have been black. Oh my, it must have been another Ikoyi in Ibadan! Methinks that was one thing his women loved about him, I suppose without exception, though I really did not interview them all for this work or interviewed any at all but one, the living senior wife at the tail end of this book.

But once, Daddy Frank used a dirty word and described a lady as ugly! I guess you would want to know how this came about. But first, I should quickly say, he did not do it in the lady's presence, but after she was out of sight and you wouldn't know Daddy Frank was mad the whole two hours or so. This lady was around us all. It was when Patrick-Oris was to go to Hamburg, Germany, for further studies. At the time, two of his elder brothers were already there—Henry Lisk-Moore and Irving-Ayiri Moore. Oris had brought his steady girlfriend home to go with us to the airport, which I suppose Daddy Frank never once saw before. I remember clearly that this lady brought a top and pants in a carry-on, ones she couldn't wear out of her parents' home. She came in a regular dress to change in our home before we all escorted Patrick-Oris to the airport. Yet on returning home, Daddy Frank blurted out that Oris took such an ugly —— to the airport! Poor Daddy. I guess he wanted a more beautiful lady as a future daughter-in-law.

Has anyone, in particular, my readers outside Africa or Nigeria heard about Ikenne? It is a town in the Ogun State of Nigeria not far from Lagos State, which the whole world knows pretty well. Really, it is not a very big town like Ijebu Ode, Shagamu, etc., in the state or as big as Abeokuta, the state capital. Yet that town (or maybe it's now a city) boasts itself as the hometown of an icon—the Chief Obafemi Awolowo, the most renowned politician Nigeria ever knew, who was the architect of free education in Nigeria. But why mention Ikenne or Awolowo in the biography of an African father, who on the surface had no connection with that town or, in particular, Awolowo? Daddy Frank may not have visited that town even once and certainly never audited for the federal government there as, at least in his time, there were no federal presence there to warrant his stopover there for months or even weeks or days to audit federal government income or expenditure vouchers. But from that town alone, Daddy Frank had three women, and all but one gave him offspring. One, Funmilayo, gave him the greatest number of children a woman ever gave to Franklin Moore—four. Another, named Doyin, who was in lamentation when I interviewed her about the matter, said, "It was my greatest desire to give him a son or a daughter, but it was not to be."

She then added that she really does not know if another Ikenne lady, the object of my inquiry, did bear him a child. The author later confirmed this fact from the third Ikenne lady who produced a daughter for Daddy Frank.

One thing that could also be said here was how much his women admired, loved, and wanted him above all others. Actually, I do not know what they see in him or by what means he distinguished himself. But certainly, if it was money, Daddy Frank was not even among the richest guys around, and some of these ladies were even richer than or at least as rich as he was. So it could not be said that they went after him for his money. Not to mention that some were happily married and were from well-to-do families too with children. This, however, is not to say that all or even half of his women were married. They all just loved him and wanted to have him for themselves alone. That reminds me of an ex-wife—my favorite stepmom, I should say, though all occupy the same position in this author's heart as wives of his daddy. This stepmom said, "I left not because of him, but because of the women in his life. I wanted to maintain my sanity!"

It was while out of the Moore home that she gave birth to her only child with Daddy Frank, the child whom I wrote about elsewhere, who resembles him the most (see picture exhibits). It was either she wanted to preserve another pregnancy she just had or she just moved out, not knowing she had taken in!

The very last thing that should not be forgotten about this man is his profound humility and reverence to God and man. To enable you to understand this more, a reference is made to an American lady who was talking to God once upon a time. In fairness to her, she has just had a fairly rough day as her sister was getting married the next day and had been very busy with the preparation. Hear what she said to God.

"That was mean of you, God,"[1] she said aloud again, as she finally turned the Peugeot into the gravel drive of the courthouse. "You really had it for me today, didn't you?" FO will never say such a thing, not even to man and especially to God Almighty. He was very respectful and meek to all, even to people much younger than him, those who were less educated, and those who may be in humbler life positions. I never knew any problem he had with his dad, but if there were any, I guess it would have been the dad not being proud of him in only one aspect of his life, which must have been that he was too easygoing. You need to know a little about Sir William Moore to understand that. I hope you still remember how the name Moore came about. A white man was with Great Granddad Akinbo when his son, black Akpieyi, came around to say something to his dad and left. But this white man was so taken aback by the stark resemblance or was surprised by the mannerism and resemblance of this black little boy to that of a white man back home in England and did not fail to mention this fact to Chief Akenbo, the boy's father, the man he was talking to before his son briefly came to him and left!

Within three years after MD and this author arrived in America, we were attending a black village church at the time. And even in church, people do not talk. They just followed the worship service along. Sunday school was for different ages and sexes, at least for adults where we both belong to. A black lady who saw us only in church came and said to us after church one Sunday that we didn't look like a couple to her, but like siblings, children of the same parents! I never heard that before in all my life. But upon reflection, I see some truth in that, although this American lady never met Daddy Frank, who was dead before we relocated and even never came to America all his life. He and Granddaddy William did not have to come to the United States since it was to the United Kingdom, not United States, that they were conversant, each as a British-protected child.[2] But MD and Daddy Frank are both so cool and quite unlike this author, Granddaddy William, or even Mummy Alice. Above all on Daddy Frank: This is not directly related to the story of my father, but should the US Congress decide to amend a section of US laws, it should be the one that debars some American citizens from running for the highest office of the land—that of the presidency. Who knows? Daddy Frank could one day be described as the father of a US president, especially as the very sons and daughters of this lineage appear to do things that make their daddy proud. A typical example would be William Moore to his father Akenbo. So far, this class of citizens in the United States that cannot contest for the presidency could still run for other offices in the land like that of senate, as well as governor position, etc., and so should...

REFERENCES

1 Vincenzi, Penny. *Another Woman*. Great Britain: Orion. pp 9, lines 8–10.

2 Achebe, Chinua. 2009. *The Education of a British-Protected Child*: *Essays*. A. Knopf.

3 Amplified Bible. 2 Sam 12:8, 1 Kings 2: 6, 9.

Printed in the United States
By Bookmasters